THE SURRENDERED WILL

AN INVITATION BACK TO THE GARDEN

DANNY ORTIZ & PETER DEWITT

TABLE OF CONTENTS

HONOR &
ACKNOWLEDGEMENTS

From Danny

I want to thank my Father in heaven for loving me, Jesus for saving me and the Holy Spirit for leading me to truth. I want to thank my wife Debbie for all the years of love and support; you are my rock and I am thankful daily that I get to spend my life with you. To my three beautiful daughters, Makayla, Malia and Maya: I am so proud of you. I never could have imagined God would give me the opportunity and privilege of fathering three incredible young women. You girls are amazing and you keep my heart beating daily. To my mom, dad, siblings and all my nieces and nephews: thank you for being my foundation. I love you all and I appreciate you for who you are in my life. To Michael and Achea: thank you for being my best friends and a bedrock of love. To Peter and Megan: I love you guys and this project would not have come to pass without you both. To every one of my friends, mentors, teachers, pastors and all those who have influenced me along the way — there are too many to name — please know that I am grateful and love you with all my heart.

From Peter

I want to thank my wife, Megan, for leading me to Jesus on March 15, 2005. I want to thank Jesus for bringing me to my Father and Holy Spirit for leading me, comforting, and empowering me every day. I want to thank my father and mother — what precious examples you have both been to me in humility and a willingness to always learn and grow. I want to thank Gary and Lorraine for training up such a beautiful daughter in the Lord and being examples to us in your devotion to God. I want to thank Brad and Mark for your loving mentorship; few have had the sort of mentorship that you both have provided me in the Lord. I want to thank my Agathos family; you all are precious to me and I am so thankful for all the blessing, love, and encouragement you strengthen me with daily. I want to thank Danny for being such a gift to me personally and for knowing it was time for this book to come forth. Finally, to my four sons, Peter, Andrew, David and William: I love you boys!

From Both of Us

Both of us also wish to thank Sarah Augenstein for designing the cover of this book; we're so grateful for your ability to take the purpose of this work and present it clearly to others. We also both want to thank Jeremy Mangerchine for his guidance in bringing this to print — your encouragement and exhortation have been invaluable. Derrick, thanks as always for your technical assistance with fonts and layout. Finally, a huge thanks to Megan, Aaron MacCaughey, and Beth DeWitt for their thorough and profoundly helpful edits; you each brought greater clarity and excellence to this book!

Throughout, direct Scripture quotes will be *italicized*. Some portions of Scripture quotes are also ***bolded for emphasis***. Sections of Scripture that are paraphrased are in plain text to clearly differentiate them from directly quoted verses. For readability and reference, Scripture references will be end-noted and organized by chapter at the end of the book.

INTRODUCTION

Jesus Sent Them out Two by Two

*"After these things the Lord appointed seventy others also, and sent them **two by two** before His face into every city and place where He Himself was about to go."* [1]

It has been an honor to write this book together out of a place of relationship. The entire book is written from our voice together – not as separate chapters from separate authors. We believe that God is establishing and releasing revelation from the foundation of relationship in this hour. We have said "yes" to this invitation and journey.

Saying "Yes" to This Message

We have also said "yes" to this message of the surrendered will. Like Ezekiel, God gave us something to eat before He gave us something to speak:

"And He said to me, 'Son of man, feed your belly, and fill your stomach with this scroll that I give you.' So I ate, and it was in my mouth like honey in sweetness.

***Then** He said to me: 'Son of man, go to the house of Israel and speak with My words to them.'"* [2]

Our goal in sharing this message is simply to be genuinely helpful. Please know that if a word in this book pierces you, it has pierced our hearts first.

It's the Glory of Kings to Search a Matter Out

This book is meant to be a map of sorts, describing a possible territory or lay of the land. And just as a map is not the actual land that it represents — only a tool to help with discovery of the real country — this book is to help you discover the surrendered life that says continually, "Not my will, but Yours be done."

As you read through this book, take your time in that discovery process. Give Holy Spirit room to speak to you. Linger in meditating on the scriptures in each section. Our purpose in having knowledge is to let it bring us closer to knowing the God who created us — to choose the Tree of Life, not the Tree of the Knowledge of Good and Evil. To have eternal life; to know God. [3]

So many of us have been (and are being) transformed by the renewing of our minds. [4] But our individual wills being conformed to His will requires us to lay down our lives in order to find them. We each must walk out our salvation with fear and trembling.[5]

We lay the message that follows before you with humility and pray that Holy Spirit would meet you in it just as He's met us.

- Danny and Peter

FOREWORD

God Redeems All Things

Jesus is our loving Redeemer. He takes the bad and exchanges it for good. He gives us beauty for ashes, joy for mourning, a garment of praise for heaviness.[1] It is the Father's delight to perfect us in relationship with Him. We see the redemptive work of God throughout all of scripture, but I want to highlight a few particular accounts.

In John 18:18, the disciple Peter stood and warmed himself by *"a fire of coals."* Just a short time prior to this scene he had told Jesus that he would never leave Him. Peter was ready to follow up on that vow; when Christ was betrayed in the garden, Peter struck the high priest's servant.[2] Peter was willing to follow Jesus anywhere and be associated with Him when he thought following Jesus looked like ruling and being the best. After Jesus tells Peter to put his sword away, we see that Peter is not as eager to follow Christ down the path of surrender. It's the same initial disbelief that Peter showed when Jesus chose servanthood and surrender in washing His disciples' feet.

While Jesus is being questioned by the high priest about His disciples and His doctrine, Peter is being questioned by a servant girl about Jesus.[3] Three times Peter denies Jesus as he warms himself by *"a fire of coals."* The Greek word for coals in that verse is *anthrakiá*. There is only one other time *anthrakiá* is used in the New Testament; John 21:9 where Jesus meets the disciples on the shore of Galilee with fish and bread on *"a fire of coals."* For Peter, seeing Jesus by this fire must have so clearly and sharply brought up the experience of denying Christ. Jesus brings Peter back to the place of failure, but this time Jesus is with him in that place and He reinstates Peter. The purpose of bringing Peter back to that place of failure is not to condemn him; instead, it's to help Peter understand in humility where his heart was — something Jesus knew the whole time. Christ was not surprised by Peter's betrayal! In fact, He redeems Peter in that place. After reinstating Peter, Jesus says to him, *"Follow me."*[4] This time, Peter is ready to follow Jesus down the path of humility and surrender.

In another story of redemption, after Christ's resurrection, Mary Magdalene is the first to see our risen Lord.[5] The name Mary is derived from Miriam (Egyptian), meaning "beloved", or Mara (Hebrew) meaning "to be rebellious or disobedient." Here Christ is revealed to a woman who then tells the disciples about the good news of the resurrection! The beloved but rebellious Eve in the Garden of Eden is tempted to believe that God is a withholder and so she takes and eats from the Tree of the Knowledge of Good and Evil. After she tastes this fruit she gives it to Adam to eat. Eve brings a bad report to Adam in the garden and brings death to all mankind.[6] Jesus redeems the disobedience of Eve and restores women by allowing Mary Magdalene to be the first bearer of the good news of the Living Christ — the Tree of Life.

God's redemption is also displayed so perfectly in the garden of Gethsemane where we witness Jesus as He lays down His own will to do the will of the Father.[7] Jesus does what the first Adam could not; lay down His own will and trust that the will of His Father was good and that it would produce good for all mankind. Through the first Adam, sin and death entered in for all humanity. Through the surrendered will of the second Adam – Christ – holiness and eternal life was made available for all humanity.

The first miracle that Christ ever performed was to turn water into wine.[8] I love this story. Every time I hear it I am reminded that when Jesus does a miracle in our lives he redeems a situation so fully that what He provides is so much better than the thing which was lost. The wine that He made was superior to the wine that had been served first. When Jesus redeems, the latter is better than the former.

God is one who restores, and He does that thoroughly. The Father took Peter back to the fire of coals where he denied Jesus and then Peter takes care of Jesus' sheep. Jesus shows up to Mary — and now a woman is the first one who brings the good news to mankind where Eve's words had brought death. Jesus goes to the garden to surrender His will as the second Adam in order to redeem all mankind at the point of separation where the first Adam chose his own will over the Father's. When we surrender our will to the Father, He restores us.

Our Redeemer lives,

Megan DeWitt

"For it is God who works in you both to will and to do for His good pleasure."

(Phil. 2:13)

1

GOD IS WORKING IN THE WILL OF HIS PEOPLE

He's Reinstating Garden Living

J esus said unto His disciples "*My soul is exceedingly sorrowful, even to death. Stay here and watch with Me.*"[1]

In the beginning, man went from the Garden of Eden into the wilderness.[2] Jesus passed through that wilderness successfully and had arrived back to a garden, but this time the Garden of Gethsemane.[3, 4]

However, He had not come back to the Garden alone; He had brought His disciples, Peter, James, and John with Him. He had already been transfigured in front of them.[5] Now He was going to be **surrendered** before their eyes:

"*O My Father, if it is possible, let this cup pass from Me; nevertheless, not as I will, but as You will.*"[6]

Jesus was reinstating garden living by surrendering His will to His Father, and He is inviting us into the same.

Sleeping Through the Test

Then He came to the disciples and found them sleeping.[7]

In the time of the fight, they were sleeping. This was not a fight against others, but of fighting with the flesh. A battle for the will was at hand. Jesus perceived it, but His disciples did not yet.

"Watch and pray, lest you enter into temptation. The spirit indeed is willing, but the flesh is weak."[8]

Church, don't sleep in the fight of your flesh. Don't let the enemy lull you to sleep when you're supposed to be saying "no" to your flesh. The lullaby of the enemy is distractions. We can get so caught up in busyness and distractions. Distractions aren't always bad things happening to you; distractions are whatever causes you to be spiritually asleep.

And God wants to awaken us.

God is saying to the worldwide church, "Awaken, there's an awakening happening! Awaken to watch and see what I am doing!"

It's the clamor of all the other things of life that lulls us to sleep spiritually. Spiritual awakening requires stillness. God's saying, *"Be still and know that I am God."*[9] There's a stillness of heart that God is asking for.

Linger a Little Longer

Jesus' disciples were sleeping and He said to Peter, *"What! Could you not watch with Me one hour?"* [10]

In Exodus we see Moses meeting with God, but the word says Joshua lingered a little longer! [11] God was training the next generation like this: "If you don't get the intellect, if you don't get the revelation, get the lingering!"

We are so used to rushing that we rush through moments with God. It's easy to go to the next thing. God is trying to pull on the reins and say "Can you linger a little longer? Can you make an art of lingering?"

Jesus is calling to His bride earnestly, *"Watch with Me."* Brothers and sisters, can we purpose in our hearts to live like this: "I am going to posture myself just to watch and see."

Jesus had made an art of lingering long before Gethsemane. In Mark 1:35, we read *"Now in the morning, having risen a long while before daylight, He (Jesus) went out and departed to a solitary place; and there He prayed. And Simon and those who were with Him searched for Him."*

Imagine the prayers of our Lord: "Father, I want to see what You're doing. I want to linger at the masterpiece that You're creating, Abba. I can do nothing of Myself, but what I **see** You do **Father**; for whatever You do Father, I also will do in like manner." [12] Jesus watched to **see** what the Father was doing.

We, too, must watch to see what the Father is doing. *"But we all, with unveiled face, beholding as in a mirror the glory of the Lord, are being transformed into the same image from glory to glory, just as by the Spirit of the Lord."* [13]

It's a beautiful thing when we receive a revelation, but too often we think, "Oh I'm getting a revelation to give to somebody else." We must realize that the revelation of God is meant to change us first!

Linger long enough that the revelation can be a part of who **you** are! Become acquainted with the revelation for **your** life! Don't let the Word of God pass through you without allowing it to transform you on its way to someone else.

It's not first for somebody else.

When God speaks to you, it's an invitation for you to sit with Him and allow Him to transform you in His presence! God's Word requires His presence. We must abide in Him **and** allow His Words to abide in us. [14] Choose to linger a little longer.

Jesus' Will Needed Work

Jesus prayed three times in the Garden. The first time He prayed:

"O My Father, if it is possible, let this cup pass from Me; nevertheless, not as I will, but as You will." [15]

He must have received His answer because His next two prayers changed:

"O My Father, if this cup cannot pass away from Me unless I drink it, Your will be done." [16]

Jesus discovered the will of the Father, but He still needed to **pray** — because His will needed work!

Just because you have heard the word of God doesn't mean you have the will of God. Just because you see the cup doesn't mean you're going to choose to partake of it. Just because we **know** doesn't mean we will **do**!

We have to **choose** His will over ours!

Just because you see the prophetic vision, just because you see the dream, just because you see it in the Word, doesn't mean you are going to partake of it, unless you surrender your will to get there! You can only drink the cup when you surrender to the cup!

We often want to skip over the surrender. We can mentally assent to the vision. We can acknowledge what we see in the Word, but can we be honest? We want to avoid this conversation, but can we be plain? Doesn't our will need some work?

Jesus Himself **needed to** pray "not My will, Father ... but Yours be done."

Is it any surprise that we need to do the same?

God is working in the
will of His people.

2

IT'S A CHOICE

"Jesus, I'm not Ready to Go Where You Are Taking Me!"

Jesus told His disciples, "Remain here, keep your eyes open and I'm going a little further."[1] The disciples were not ready to go where He was going.

We have to be honest with ourselves. "Jesus, I know where you're taking me, but sometimes I'm not ready to go where You're going. I'm still dealing with some things."

Jesus' prayer of surrender was not for Him alone. It remains a model for us. God-in-the-flesh prayed three times about the cup He was to drink![2] If it was important for Him to spend time in this type of prayer to see the Lord's will accomplished, then as God calls us into our prayer closets and back into the Garden, this must be our prayer too!

Revival can't happen; awakening can't happen; the oneness with the Father that Jesus talked about can't happen — unless the prayer of surrender marks our hearts.

Sustainable Oneness

A heart-stance or attitude of surrendering our will to the Father is the gateway to sustainable oneness.

We're not talking about oneness just for Sunday services or worship nights.

We're not talking about oneness just when we pray in our prayer closet.

We're talking about sustainable oneness in which we are constantly one with the Father, Son and the Holy Spirit. Sustainable oneness is remaining in Him, abiding in Him and letting His words abide in us.[3]

"But, how?"

Through surrender.

In Matthew 6, Jesus teaches us to pray. He says, first recognize your identity: "I'm a son, You're my Father." Then worship: "Hallowed be Your name." Then pray: "Your kingdom come and Your will be done on Earth."[4]

The prayer for disciples is for **the Father's will** to be done on earth as it is in Heaven.

Garden living is where He's calling us. There is a oneness that we have not yet known, but oneness cannot begin unless there's a death.

Becoming One Flesh Requires Two Deaths

In Genesis 2 and again in Matthew 19, we see that when a man and woman marry, the two become one. Jesus said, *"a man shall leave his father and mother and be joined to his wife, and the two shall become one flesh?' So then, they are no longer two but* **one** *flesh."* [5, 6]

The only way to oneness is for both sides to die to who they thought they were at the time so that they can become a new, singular, **one**.

Both sides.

The man has to say, "I'm dead." The woman has to say, "I'm dead." Then, when they come together they become someone new.

Likewise in the kingdom the two — the Son and His Bride — shall become **one**![7] But it takes surrender. Surrender of our independence, of our own will. **Surrender is the gateway to sustainable oneness**.

On the part of the Godhead, His work is done! He gave the sacrifice of His Son![8]

Guess what He's waiting for?

He is waiting for you to die to yourself so that you can become one with Him.[9] He's waiting for your death. A lot of times we're not progressing in oneness because a part of us is still trying to remain alive.

Jesus made His choice to be one with you. John 10 says, *"Therefore My Father loves Me, because I lay down My life that I may take it again. No one takes it from Me, but I lay it down of Myself."* [10]

God says, "Listen, I know how strong your will is and how strong your flesh is. And I tell you that they are at enmity with your spirit, but you don't believe Me.[11] You're not seeing the fruit of my Word in areas of your life. You're not seeing the dreams I've given you come to pass. It is because you haven't yet settled it in your will. You haven't yet surrendered."

God is Working in Our Wills

We have heard many sermons on the transformative power of renewing our mind.[12] Many of us have also learned not to be led by our emotions.[13] But our mind and emotions are only two out of the three parts of our soul.

God is also working in our wills.

Paul knew this; *"Therefore, my beloved, as you have always obeyed, not as in my presence only, but now much more in my absence, work out your own salvation with fear and trembling; for **it is God who works in you both to will** and to do for His good pleasure."* [14]

God is working in us to will what He wills. But you can't **learn** surrender. You have to **choose** it.

"Not my will, but Yours be done."

It's a choice.

Our ability to choose is powerful. God will never override our wills; they have to be surrendered.

He's never going to make us do anything. He did not create robots; He created man and He put a will in man.

God had faith in man before man could have faith in God. Essentially, His word reveals this progression: "I'm going to put will in man, and then I'm going to have faith that man is going to come back to Me."

This is what we see in the garden fight. Jesus in the flesh had a will different than God's and He **chose** to surrender it back to His Father.[15]

It's a choice.

3

KNOWING GOD IS NOT A MEANS TO ANOTHER END

Complaining and Disputing

Directly after Paul says *"it is God who works in you both to will and to do for His good pleasure,"* he continues with:

*"Do all things without **complaining** and **disputing**, that you may become blameless and harmless, children of God without fault in the midst of a crooked and perverse generation, among whom you shine as lights in the world ..."* [1]

Complaining and disputing within the Body of Christ are fruit of un-surrendered wills.

What we each cannot endure without an attitude of complaining indicates a part in each of us that has not yet died. Dead people don't get offended.

"I Have to Find What Makes Me Happy"

"Where do wars and fights come from among you?" James asks us. *"Do they not come from your desires for pleasure that war in your members?"* [2]

The sentiment of "I have to find **me**. I have to find what makes **me** happy" often drives our lives.

Happiness is not the end purpose of Christianity. You may find that idea offensive, but happiness is not the goal of Christianity. Will you be happy in the end? Yes, but that is a result, not the purpose.

Our focus, and the ultimate outcome, is oneness with the Father.

Some of us have been listening to too much psychology that focuses on a message of personal happiness and the need to find what makes us happy.

That ideology claims, "I have to find the people that make me happy. I'm going to surround myself with people that are like-minded." Such a mindset goes against the reality that sometimes God's going to put people in your life who will kill your flesh in certain areas because your flesh needs to be killed in those areas. You don't need to cut those people off, you need to let God cut out the part of you that can't be at peace with all men. [3]

Saturated in Humility

Oneness with God requires submitting your will to Him. Oneness with God is saying, "God, I know you've given me the power to have my own will, but I'm surrendering it back to You. I want You to be my power."

Are God's passions your passions? When you hear another shopper at the local store talking with someone about Jesus, is your reaction, "My goodness, they also know Him like I know Him! They also want Him like I want Him?"

When you walk into someone's home and they have worship playing, do you pause and say, "Hold on, I've got to worship. There's worship here!"

David's words show us that if we aren't delighted to hear others worship, it is evidence of pride. *"My soul shall make its boast in the Lord; the **humble** shall hear of it and be glad."* [4]

God's dwelling place is with the humble. *"For thus says the High and Lofty One Who inhabits eternity, Whose name is Holy: 'I dwell in the high and holy place, with him who has a contrite and humble spirit, to revive the spirit of the humble, and to revive the heart of the contrite ones.'"* [5]

Jesus says, *"Blessed are the poor in spirit, for theirs is the kingdom of heaven."* [6]

We need to be **saturated in humility**.

We so often have an attitude that says, "I've done that before. I've been in that service before. I've heard that kind of preaching before. Let them worship. I'm cool."

No.

That's called arrogance; that is pride.

We need the revelation of humility so that whenever someone sings about Jesus, our first response is not, "I sang that song before," but instead, "Where can I lay my face?"

Follow Your Passions?

Much of the body of Christ has struggled with the question of whether or not to teach people to follow their passions. The issue, however, is with the order of operations.

Many believers try to find passion for God's work when what they haven't yet found is surrender to His will.

Before trying to find and fulfill your passion, you have to ask, "Have I found my surrender?"

"For whoever desires to save his life will lose it, but whoever loses his life for My sake will save it." [7]

God is in the business of resurrecting that which is laid down. Submit your entire will, surrender your entire world to God, and you'll be allowed to pursue what God puts in front of you because your passion will be His passion, and His passion will be your passion — this is the epitome of oneness.

"Delight yourself also in the Lord, and He shall give you the desires of your heart." [8]

Additive Christianity

The Spirit of God is saying, "When Jesus becomes a religion instead of a relationship, it results in additive Christianity instead of sustainable oneness."

God desires oneness. He desires relationship. [9]

Additive Christianity desires Him in order to earn or access something. Yes, God is a rewarder of those who diligently seek Him, **but** the purpose of knowing Him is not to sustain religion; it's not to sustain Christianity. [10]

Instead He's asking, "Will you be sons and daughters of the King and be one with Abba through the Son, and the Holy Spirit?" God desires sustainable oneness.

Oneness that is not for you to achieve something.

Oneness that is not for you to prove something.

Oneness that is not for you to be acceptable to others.

Oneness that is not a means of some other gain.

Godliness is **not** a means of gain. [11]

But Godliness with contentment **is** great gain. [12]

God is telling His church, "You can have oneness today." He is inviting us back to the Garden to walk with Him in the

21

cool of the day for no other reason than to hear what He has to say. God desires that sort of oneness. He desires that sort of relationship. But additive Christianity desires Him in order to earn or access something else — sometimes even a good something else.

Jesus said there's a wicked and adulterous generation that seeks after a sign.[13] Signs and wonders are wonderful, but they are not the glory we seek. Jesus also said there are those who teach on their own authority in order to seek their own glory.[14] Doctrine is essential, but it is not the glory we seek. The glory Jesus is giving to us is showing us how to have relationship, how to have oneness, with the Father!

*"And the glory which You gave Me I have given them, **that they may be one just as We are one**: I in them, and You in Me; that they may be made perfect in one."* [15]

From Doing to Burning

Relationship with the Father and Son is the end result. *"And this is **eternal life**, that they may know You, the only true God, and Jesus Christ whom You have sent."* [16]

Jesus promised, *"If anyone loves Me, he will keep My word; and My Father will love him, and We will come to him and make Our home with him."* [17]

We are going back to Genesis 1 — perfectly one in the garden. Our destination is intimacy.

"I in them, and You in Me; that they may be made perfect in one, and that the world may know that You have sent Me, and have loved them as You have loved Me." [18] The world will see when we surrender, when we walk in oneness.

But we often think "Let's do. I have to **show** them Jesus. I have to **convince** them of Jesus. I have to **do** Evangelism 101."

If you walk in oneness, there is no Evangelism 101. The world will see it on you and in you, at which point you just get to be a lamp on a stand. [19]

The enemy is beating us up by trying to get us to do things for God instead of resting in oneness with God.

"One thing I have desired of the Lord, that will I seek: that I may dwell in the house of the Lord all the days of my life, to behold the beauty of the Lord, and to inquire in His temple." [20]

We don't want additive Christianity; we want sustainable oneness. And in order to walk in oneness, we have to seek the face of God. We cannot skip the process of spending time in the presence of the Lord.

Knowing God is not a means to another end.

Paul says, *"But **what things were gain to me, these I have counted loss for Christ.** Yet indeed I also count all things loss for **the excellence of the knowledge of Christ Jesus my Lord**, for whom I have suffered the loss of all things, and count them as rubbish, that I may gain Christ."* [21] No other thing compares with gaining Christ!

May we be awakened with fire and no longer distracted by other desires. We need daily encounters with Jesus. Pastors, preachers: your flock doesn't need an encounter with your words. Worship leaders, congregants don't need us to sing pretty songs. They need encounters with Jesus Himself!

Yes, God is going to partner with you, and yes, God is going to do great things through you. But, miracles and signs and wonders are not the thing. Your pretty singing or powerful preaching is not what's going to sustain them in their hour of trouble. They must know Jesus for themselves! They must know a living Savior and burn with fire for Him! We need the fire that John the Baptist refers to in Luke 3:16, *"One mightier than I is coming, whose sandal strap I am not worthy to loose. He will baptize you with the Holy Spirit and fire."* We need that baptism.

Paul needed to count all things loss to gain Christ. Holy Spirit is again inviting us to *"Turn at my rebuke; Surely I will pour out my spirit on you; I will make my words known to you."* [22]

Knowing God is not a
means to another end.

4

IT'S BETWEEN YOU AND GOD

Whatever I Command You

"*You are My friends if you do whatever I command you.*"[1]

Why have we lost this?

God is restoring the fear of the Lord to His church and it looks like surrender.

He wants to make His word known to us. His desire is to refresh His bride with good words. But the words you expect to hear are often not the words you most need to hear.

When Jesus multiplied food for the 5,000, He told His disciples to *"Gather up the fragments that remain, so that nothing is lost."*[2]

It was **after** they picked up the fragments that remained that they saw the miracle that Jesus had done.[3] The crowd ate and was satisfied, but Jesus further directed them, "What remains is still important. Your miracle is **in** what you didn't eat the first time I set it in front of you. Don't let it go to waste!"

There's a certain type of food that they expected, that they were hungry for, that they were looking for, and that they ate the first time He set it in front of them; but the other food, the fragments that remained, were actually still things that Jesus had set in front of them to eat.

They just didn't know they needed those "extra pieces" at that time.

Brothers and sisters, we are being fed some pieces we didn't know that we needed. It's important to take this stance of humility and surrender: "If Jesus gave it to me, I'm going to eat it all. Even the things that don't seem appetizing, even the things that I thought I didn't need, even the things I wasn't looking for."

"You are My friends if you do whatever I command you."[1]

Prophetically Blinded

God caused Saul to be blinded so that Saul could start to see correctly.

Immediately after Jesus said *"You are My friends if you do whatever I command you,"* He said *"No longer do I call you servants, for a servant does not know what his master is doing; but I have called you friends, for all things that I heard from My Father I have made known to you."*[4]

Humility is the key of knowledge.[5]

In one of his letters, Peter marveled at Paul's revelation but remember that Paul was first Saul and Saul had to say, "Lord, I surrender. What do you want me to do?" [6, 7]

It was an encounter with heaven that shifted the opinion of Saul to say, "What in the world am I doing?" Saul had recognized that Jesus is Lord, but in Acts 9, Saul recognized that he was not submitted to Him! [8]

"But why do you call Me 'Lord, Lord,' and not do the things which I say?" [9]

Saul had to go through a metamorphosis. His eyes were blinded and he could not see for a little while.[10]

The physical blindness allowed Saul to see his own spiritual blindness.

That's Between You and God

God wants each of his children to hear Him directly.[11]

God's inviting His church back to hearing Him one-on-one. Hearing **about** God is not the same as hearing **from** Him.

The doctrine of the Nicolaitans will always cause people to desire to hear through another person; but to *"him who overcomes I will give some of the hidden manna to eat. And I will give him a white stone, and on the stone a new name written which no one knows except him who receives it."* [12, 13]

Every person gets a white stone and on that white stone is a name that is written that no one aside from God knows! Why? Because it's only out of the place of intimacy with God that the name is written and no one else knows what it is — only you and Him do!

That's between you and God.

"I will be their God, and they shall be My people. None of them shall teach his neighbor, and none his brother, saying, 'Know the Lord,' for all shall know Me, from the least of them to the greatest of them." [14]

The first word "know" here means to "know intellectually" whereas the second word for "know" implies seeing with your own eyes! In other words, in the New Covenant, none of them shall teach his neighbor, and none his brother, saying, "Know about the Lord intellectually," for all shall see Him with their own eyes, from the least of them to the greatest of them!

Every believer is called to be a witness, and witnesses, by definition, have to have seen something with their own eyes! [15] Lingering in intimacy is what produces eyewitness testimonies.

Jesus didn't die for second-hand friendship with you.

You Can't Teach the Surrendered Will

For God to do a deep work in the will of His church, each of us must hear from Him directly and specifically. Hearing **about** God is not the same as hearing **from** Him.

When we **teach** the fear of the Lord, we are left to describe it as principles, but we can't actually teach the surrendered will.

We can't even preach the surrendered will.

We can't surrender someone's will for them.

For God to do a deep work in the will of His church, each of us must hear from Him directly and specifically.

*"For it is **God** who works in you both to will and to do for His good pleasure."* [16]

God has taken some of His ministers off of platforms so they can observe for a while. Many believers are not perceiving this shift in season and are still asking those ministers all their questions. The platform has shifted. The teaching of truth is imperative, but *"they overcame him by the blood of the Lamb and by the word of their testimony."* [17] God is telling those ministers with ears to hear "Don't give the answer; share some testimony."

"Just Say 'yes' to What I am Doing"

As individuals, when we first realize God is working in our wills, the sorts of things that will be made visible in our hearts may disturb us. We may think, "How can I think like that? I know better than that." But that's a trap. A person's will is not a "thinker" but a "decider."

God's not exposing your thinking; He's revealing your purposes.

Powerful encounters get past what we understand, which is essential, because we often understand according to our will.[18, 19]

The will dictates our deep thoughts and judgments; as a man thinks in His heart so is He.[20]

In some areas of our life, we can't get to a transformed mind, because we don't yet have a surrendered will in that area. The will is dominating the intellect so more information or even more understanding cannot override a determined will.[19]

Only God's presence can.

Paul was **convinced** that killing Christians was God's will.[21] He could not see past that. His powerful encounter with God finally allowed his intellect to see God's will.[10]

In 1 Corinthians 4, Paul said he was not coming to hear their words, but to see their power.[22] The gentleness of God is welling up within Him to set us free, but many of us are still struggling to submit to the work He's doing in our hearts because we don't have words for it yet and we wonder if it lines up with our theology and judgments.

God is saying "Just say 'yes' to what I am doing. What I am doing is a new thing, so if you try to figure it out through an existing lens you will say 'no' to it, and, likewise, if you try to self-promote yourself into it, you won't end up in what I've actually prepared for you."

Each of us will give an account to God.[23] Your pastor is not responsible to surrender your will. Your parents are not responsible to surrender your will. Your friends are not responsible to surrender your will. When God is speaking to your heart, your "yes" is yours alone to give.

It's between you and God.

5

IT IS GOD WHO WORKS IN YOU TO WILL

He Will Satisfy You

"*He satisfies the longing soul, and fills the hungry soul with goodness.*"[1]

There is a longing we have had in our souls. Perhaps for acceptance, significance, or security. It's slightly different for every one of us. But that longing has become a motivator and that motivator has become a strong will within us.

When God begins to work in our wills, it can be a confusing season because we think "I thought God wanted me to hold onto His promises, to speak in faith, to prophecy, to preach, to seek revelation, and so on."

But God has His finger on certain things in our hearts.

He's not asking us to surrender His promises, or prophecy, or preaching. No, those are beautiful things. He's asking us to surrender the ambition; to surrender the drive; to surrender the un-submitted will; to surrender those things that steal our peace.

"Rejoice always, pray without ceasing, in everything give thanks; **for this is the will of God** *in Christ Jesus for you."* [2] Being able to rejoice at all times, being able to have an on-going conversation with God, and being able to give thanks in everything — these abilities are evidence of surrendering to His will in our lives.

If you have a longing in your soul that causes you to grumble instead of rejoicing always, if you have a desire that you can't talk with God about openly, if you often see lack instead of giving thanks in everything, know that He will fill your hungry soul with His goodness. An un-surrendered will quenches the Spirit, distorts our approach to prophecy (causing us to either despise it or to not test it), and makes us susceptible to certain temptations. [3]

God sees your need. He sees your longing. He sees what steals your peace.

The God of Peace Himself wants to sanctify you completely so that your whole spirit, soul, and body may be preserved blameless at the coming of our Lord Jesus Christ. He who calls you is faithful; He will do it! [4]

You can cast that need upon Him and He will care for it for you! [5]

He will satisfy you. He will satisfy the longing. He will fill your soul with goodness.

Surrender is not a Work

Oneness and surrender are not a work. They are a response to His goodness. They are not achieved apart from God through our self-effort; they are received in His presence.

In John 6, people asked Christ, *"What shall we do, that we may work the works of God?"* [6] Our job description hung in the balance of Jesus' answer.

He replied with perfect simplicity, *"Believe in Him whom He sent."* [7]

Jesus' words still encapsulate the job description of every one of God's children.

When we step into greater surrender and intimacy with the Lord, we can feel as though we need to maintain it through some sort of perfection; but the Lord says, "Having begun in the Spirit, are you now being made perfect by the flesh? I don't need the strength of your flesh, I just need the strength of your 'yes.'" [8]

"It is the Spirit who gives life; the flesh profits nothing." [9]

Righteousness is not accounted to us for a work, but instead for saying "yes" to what God is saying. *"Abraham **believed God**, and it was accounted to him for righteousness."* [10]

Walking According to the Spirit

Paul famously said, *"There is therefore now no condemnation to those who are in Christ Jesus, who do not walk according to the flesh, but according to the Spirit."* [11]

Many of us have read *"who do not walk according to the flesh"* as "who do not sin or do the works of the flesh." In other words, we read it as not being a fornicator, or not being an adulterer, or not being a thief, or not being a liar; but that's not what Romans 8 is talking about.

Those sinful behaviors are fruits of walking according to the flesh.[12] Jesus and Paul define walking according to the flesh as setting our minds on our strength, our performance, our obedience: *"For those who live according to the flesh set their minds on the things of the flesh, but those who live according to the Spirit, the things of the Spirit. For to be carnally minded is death, but to be spiritually minded is life and peace."* [13]

We tend to want a job description that includes our strength, our performance, and our obedience, to which Jesus says, "Believe in the One Whom He sent."

Whom did the Father send?

His Word! Jesus is the Word! *"It is the Spirit who gives life; the flesh profits nothing. **The words that I speak to you are spirit**, and they are life."* [9]

The point is this: when God begins to speak to us about something as encompassing as our need to surrender, our job is not to try to make it happen. Our job is not to constantly check the surrender of our hearts.

When Jesus is leading us to surrender, our job is simply to respond with ... "yes."

"Yes!"

Believing His Word sent to us — this is the work of God; this is walking according to the Spirit.[14] *"There is therefore now no condemnation to those who are in Christ Jesus, **who do not walk according to the flesh, but according to the Spirit**."*[11]

It is God Who Works

"God so loved the world that He gave ..."[15]

Notice the nouns.

God is the subject. He is the lover. We, the world, are the recipients of His love. We love because He first loved us.

Again, Philippians 2:13 says, *"For **it is God who works** in you both to will and to do for His good pleasure."* Notice the nouns again. Who is doing the work in you both to will and to do for His good pleasure?

God!

Romans 8:13 says, *"If **by the Spirit** you put to death the deeds of the body, you will live."* It is **only** by the Spirit that you can put to death the deeds of the flesh.

"The spirit indeed is willing, but the flesh is weak." [16]

Thankfully, Holy Spirit has all the willingness we will ever need. The will is there for God, but our flesh needs help even surrendering to that. Holy Spirit says, "don't try willpower; try surrender! I've empowered you to die to that flesh. I've given you the power to say 'yes.'"

Even faith is a gift from God so that no one may boast. [17]

It is God who works in you both to will and to do for His good pleasure!

Responding to His Love

Oneness and surrender are not a work, but a response to His love. What if God's truth ministered to you only for freedom — not for acceptance?

If you have accepted Christ's work on the cross, you are a child of God. [18] As a child of God, you are **already accepted** in the Beloved. *"He chose us in Him before the foundation of the world, that we should be holy and without blame before Him in love, having predestined us to adoption as sons by Jesus Christ to Himself, according to the good pleasure of His will, to the praise of the glory of His grace, by which He made us accepted in the Beloved."* [19]

When God knocks on a hidden door in your heart, on a place needing surrender, we can get wild inside, but the Lord says, "Do not fear. I'm not ministering truth to you so you can become a son ... I'm ministering truth to you because you already are one!"

"If you endure chastening, God deals with you as with sons; for what son is there whom a father does not chasten? But if you are without chastening, of which all have become partakers, then you are illegitimate and not sons." [20]

Sons receive chastening as an evidence of sonship, not as a work by which to achieve sonship.

"And you shall know the truth, and the truth shall make you free." [21] When God is speaking truth into a difficult area, it is **only** for your freedom, not for your acceptance.

It's His goodness that leads us to repentance! [22]

It is God who works
in you to will.

6

WHATEVER IT IS, IT'S READILY AVAILABLE IN HIM

The Nature of Relationship

Do you clean yourself up for relationship with God?

Or do you trust the power of relationship to keep you clean?

Jesus says, *"You are already clean because of the word which I have spoken to you."* [1]

Isn't it amazing that the words our Savior has spoken to us are able to do what our works and performance will never be able to do?

"Who can say, 'I have made my heart clean, I am pure from my sin.'" [2]

Before the prodigal son came home, he thought it all through and prepared his speech: *"Father, I have sinned against heaven*

and before you, and I am no longer worthy to be called your son.
Make me like one of your hired servants." [3]

Do you see the prodigal son's train of thought: "Father, I
have sinned against you. I have hid from you. But I'm coming back ... I know I am no longer your son ... because of
what I've done."

He assumed he was no longer worthy to be called a son. He
didn't understand the nature of relationship.

Caution Tape

The messes of our life are often surrounded by caution tape
in our hearts.

"Don't go there," our hearts say.

But then God enters into your mess.

When we are not confident in God's love, we try to pre-clean
what only relationship with God can redeem.

The areas in your life where there is sin, where there is wrong
motivation, or where there is failure are the very areas where
the Father wants to meet you. [4]

We think, "When I get this cleaned up, then I can have relationship." The Father says, "Actually this is not cleaned up
because you're attempting it apart from relationship."

Do you attempt to clean yourself up for relationship? Or
do you trust the power of relationship to keep you clean?

What if your greatest place of security in the entire world is not the perfection of your flesh, but instead is the words of your Father?

Note the prescription Jesus gave Peter, James, and John in the Garden of Gethsemane: *"Watch and **pray**, lest you enter into temptation."* [5] Have communion with God. God doesn't need you to caution-tape off sections of your heart. **He** is willing to come into your mess. **He** is able to keep you from stumbling. **He** will present you blameless before the presence of His glory with great joy! [6]

God Cannot Look upon Sin?

Religion has told us that God can't look upon sin, but let's look at what the Bible says. The prophet Habakkuk asked God a question: *"You are of purer eyes than to behold evil, and cannot look on wickedness. Why **do** You look on those who deal treacherously, and hold Your tongue when the wicked devours a person more righteous than he?"* [7] Even within his question Habakkuk acknowledged that God **does** look on those who deal treacherously!

We should not base our theology on a man-made question when we have the God-given answer.

God answers Habakkuk like this: *"Write the vision and make it plain on tablets, that he may run who reads it ... the just shall live by his faith."* [8]

God said, "Let's be clear! The answer is never going to be the strength of your flesh … the just shall live by faith!" [9]

God sent His Son into the world to save sinners.[10] Jesus was born into the mess of a manger.[11] He actually became known as a **friend** of tax collectors and sinners.[12]

God sees you and loves you at your worst.

*"But God demonstrates His own love toward us, in that **while we were still sinners, Christ died for us**. Much more then, having now been justified by His blood, we shall be saved from wrath through Him."* [13]

God has demonstrated the type of love He has for you. It's the type that gave everything for you while you were yet a sinner.

Relationship with Him has never been, nor ever will be, about your performance.

He sacrificed everything for you while you were still actively rejecting Him. He chose to give up His Son to make you His son.[14] So now, having become a son, how **much more** shall you be safe from being cast off when you make a mess of something?

"You are My servant, I have chosen you and have not cast you away: fear not, for I am with you." [15]

"Adam, Where are You!?"

Remember that when Adam sinned, God went looking for him!

God was not rejecting Adam and Eve because they had sinned; He was searching again for His relationship with them.

"Adam, where are you? I can't find you." [16]

Why would the Creator of the Universe need help finding them? It's not that He didn't know where they were.

No, He wanted Adam and Eve to know where they were with Him!

He was trying to say, "I know what you've done, I know where you are, but I still love you anyway, and I'm still calling."

God is Ready to Redeem

God is ready to redeem that which is lost, that which is broken, and that which feels cast off.

God's love does not flinch when He sees your sin, but sin flinches when it sees God's love because it knows it's on its way out. [17]

"All that is in the world—the lust of the flesh, the lust of the eyes, and the pride of life—is not of the Father but is of the world." [18] The love of the Father will displace the love of the world.

The prodigal son left home seeking a party lifestyle.[19] And yet when the prodigal came home from that party lifestyle, thinking he was no longer worthy to be called a son, his Father did the unthinkable:

He threw him a party.[20]

The thing you've been trying to get apart from the Father is readily available in Him.[21]

The thing you've been trying to get apart from the Father is abundantly available in Him.[22]

The thing you've been trying to get apart from the Father is solely available in Him.[23]

Surrender is not a matter of giving something up, but of returning to your Father as your Source! God satisfies the longing soul.

God will satisfy the longing in your soul.

Whatever it is,
it is readily available in Him.

7

"EVERYTHING YOU NEED IS FOUND IN ME"

God Cares

God cares more about what you care about than you do.[1] If our earthly fathers know how to give good gifts to those who ask, *"how much more will your Father who is in heaven give good things to those who ask Him!"*[2] All things that pertain to life and godliness are available to you through Knowing Him![3]

God's name is "I AM" for a reason.[4] He is saying to you, "My child, I am Whoever you need Me to be."

Aside from your Father, no other source is necessary.

Yet, when Adam and Eve ate of the Tree of the Knowledge of Good and Evil, they partook of the lie that said, "Everything you need is **not** found in God. He is withholding something, so source it for yourself. Become your own **source**."[5]

The Tree of the Knowledge of Good and Evil

Many of us have presumed that the Tree of the Knowledge of Good and Evil was bad because it included the knowledge of evil. We are reminded of the expression "see no evil, hear no evil, speak no evil" and think "of course this tree was bad! It was the Tree of the Knowledge of Evil!"

But the Tree of the Knowledge of Good and Evil was not just bad because it included the knowledge of evil. It was also bad because it included the knowledge of good apart from God.

"The Lord God planted a garden eastward in Eden, and there He put the man whom He had formed. And out of the ground the Lord God made every tree grow that is pleasant to the sight and good for food. The tree of life was also in the midst of the garden, and the tree of the knowledge of good and evil."[6]

Notice that God had placed three types of trees in the Garden for man:

- Every tree that is pleasant to the sight and good for food
- The Tree of Life
- The Tree of the Knowledge of Good and Evil

God placed Adam and Eve in the Garden and He said to them, *"Of every tree of the garden you may freely eat; but of the tree of the knowledge of good and evil you shall not eat, for in the day that you eat of it you shall surely die."*[7]

So God said to Adam and Eve that they could eat freely of **every** tree of the garden except one: the Tree of the Knowledge of Good and Evil.

Hear this: that means they could have chosen to eat of the Tree of Life.

The Tree of Life

Jesus said, *"I am the way, the truth, and the life. No one comes to the Father except through Me."* [8] Adam and Eve were allowed to be in communion with The Life — Jesus; they were allowed to eat of the Tree of Life.

"I am the vine, you are the branches." [9]

When Adam and Eve chose The Tree of the Knowledge of Good and Evil, they chose against relationship with the Tree of Life! They chose against relationship with Christ!

The issue with the Tree of the Knowledge of Good and Evil vs. the Tree of Life is **source**; and the battle over **source** is still at hand.

Beware Lest Anyone Cheat You

In Colossians 2:8 Paul warns, *"Beware lest anyone cheat you through philosophy and empty deceit, according to the tradition of men, according to the basic principles of the world, and not according to Christ."*

The word "according to" throughout this verse is very interesting in the Greek. It is *kata* and means things like "stemming forth from, emanating from, springing forth from, etc." In short *kata* refers to **source**.

So Paul warns, "Beware lest anyone cheat you through philosophy and empty deceit that stems forth from the tradition of men, that springs forth from the basic principles of the world, and does not originate or flow forth from Christ."

Jesus teaches us in John 15 that He is the True Vine and we are the branches. What is flowing in Him will flow out of us if we abide in Him and Him in us. That is how we bear much fruit. Apart from remaining in Him, we can do nothing.[10]

The picture Christ is painting inspires the question: are you connected to the True Vine, the True Source?

Paul was warning the Colossians — thousands of years after Adam and Eve were deceived — about the same false source from which they had received. Again, the issue with the Tree of the Knowledge of Good and Evil is **source**, and the battle over **source** is still at hand.

All Good is from God

"Do not be deceived, my beloved brethren. Every good gift and every perfect gift is from above, and comes down from the Father of lights, with whom there is no variation or shadow of turning."[11]

While simple, the following is actually quite important:

58

Good is from God.

and

Everything that does not originate from God (even if it seems good to us) is **not** good.

"There is a way that seems right to a man, but its end is the way of death." [12]

The Tree of the Knowledge of Good and Evil was not bad just because it included the knowledge of evil. It was also bad because it included the knowledge of good apart from God.

The battle over **source** is still at hand.

The Rich Young Ruler

"Now behold, one came and said to Him, 'Good Teacher, what good thing shall I do that I may have eternal life?' So He said to him, 'Why do you call Me good? No one is good but One, that is, God.'" [13]

Nothing is good apart from God.

Jesus then began to address the issue of **source** in the young man's life:

"Jesus said to him, 'If you want to be perfect, go, sell what you have and give to the poor, and you will have treasure in heaven; and come, follow Me.'" [14]

"Where your treasure is, there your heart will be also." [15]

Jesus was not talking about the perfection of performance but the maturity of oneness — the **singleness of source**. God wasn't against the young man's possessions; He cared about the posture of his heart. So He gave him an opportunity to choose relationship with Him.

"But when the young man heard that saying, he went away sorrowful, for he had great possessions." [16]

He chose the possessions.

"Everything you need
is found in Me."

8

"I SURRENDER"

"You Are the Man!"

I n 2 Samuel 12, we read:

"Then the Lord sent Nathan to David. And he came to him, and said to him: 'There were two men in one city, one rich and the other poor. The rich man had exceedingly many flocks and herds. But the poor man had nothing, except one little ewe lamb which he had bought and nourished; and it grew up together with him and with his children. It ate of his own food and drank from his own cup and lay in his bosom; and it was like a daughter to him. And a traveler came to the rich man, who refused to take from his own flock and from his own herd to prepare one for the wayfaring man who had come to him; but he took the poor man's lamb and prepared it for the man who had come to him.'

So David's anger was greatly aroused against the man, and he said to Nathan, 'As the Lord lives, the man who has done this shall surely die!'" [1]

David's eyes were opened to injustice. He was starting to see from God's perspective. David declared:

"And he shall restore fourfold for the lamb, because he did this thing and because he had no pity." [2]

God is always restoring and redeeming. After hearing from Nathan, David was starting to have the Father's heart about the man with the one lamb, but much to his surprise, God was actually wanting to restore **him**!

"Then Nathan said to David, 'You are the man!'" [3]

We live in a culture where people are trying to "be the man!" But the rich man in Nathan's story wasn't the sort of man David was hoping to be. Sometimes we can hear what Heaven is saying and think that what we are hearing applies to someone else which can cause us to miss the message. [4]

Addressing Ambition

"Do not be like the horse or like the mule ... which must be harnessed with bit and bridle, else they will not come near you." [5]

Do you have untamed or unbridled ambition in your life, or do you have true contentment?

When you fall asleep at night does your heart say, "You're my Father; I'm your child; and that's enough for me?"

Or is there something more that you're constantly looking for?

"When I have _____, THEN I will have really arrived."

"When I accomplish _____, THEN I will really be someone."

"When I know/do _____, THEN people will know I am right."

The lust of the flesh, the lust of the eyes, and the pride of life always take, yet are never satisfied. They produce an unyielding drive, an ambition, for that one thing, that one moment, that one relationship, that one accomplishment, that one accolade, that perfect theology or faultless exhibition of purity that will *finally* make everything right. But it never comes. And we still feel undone.

So much of what we've prophesied to others has been tainted by ambition. So much of what we've prayed has been colored by the lust for more. So much of what we've learned has been for self-verification.

But God is inviting us back into contentment.

Godliness with contentment **is** great gain.[6]

We brought nothing into this world. We likewise will take nothing out — except our relationship with the Father.[7]

What is Success?

We have to be able to define success before we can access it.

Success is a journey, not a destination.

Success is being, and not performing.

Success is not achieving something, but is revealing something.

TRUE success is freedom.

TRUE success is contentment.

Jesus said, *"Most assuredly, I say to you, the Son can do nothing of Himself, but what He sees the Father do; for whatever He does, the Son also does in like manner."* [8]

Jesus also said, *"For I have not spoken on My own authority; but the Father who sent Me gave Me a command, what I should say and what I should speak."* [9]

God is addressing impurity even in the prophetic. Yes, His promises are still "yes and amen!" [10] Yes, He still calls those things that aren't as though they are. [11] Yes, He still has good plans for you! [12]

But He doesn't have ambition for you.

God is not consumed with what we can accomplish for Him. He knows that when we are **with** Him we will accomplish His purposes. [13]

It wasn't just David who said, "one thing I seek." [14] The Father is singularly seeking **your** heart.

Purifying Motives

The surrendered will is **singleness of source**.

God is working in our will because our motives are impure. And our motives are impure because we have more than One source.

We thought we needed that …

We thought we needed to be …

We thought we had to achieve …

But God is saying, "Just be with Me. For apart from Me, you can do nothing." [15]

The thing you've been trying to get apart from the Father is readily available in Him. The person you've been trying to be apart from the Father is already accepted in Him.

Surrender is not a matter of giving something up, but instead of returning to your Father as your only Source!

Again, God satisfies the longing soul.[16]

God will satisfy that longing in your soul.

Contentment

You may feel a weightiness or spiritual sobriety right now.

If so, know this: God is ending, for his children, the addiction to the intoxication of ambition.

The lust for more, the pride of independent achievement, and the desire for self-justification are about to surrender.

God's breathing the spirit of contentment across your heart and mind.

The peace of God is going to surpass your understanding and guard your heart and mind in Christ Jesus.[17]

This is the invitation back to the Garden.

"Not my will, but Yours be done."

"I surrender."

9

"HERE I AM, LORD …"

He Looked at Him and Loved Him

Looking again at the story of the rich young ruler, we see that Jesus was sharing truth with him so that he could be free — not so that he could become lovable.

Consider Jesus' disposition when He spoke to him:

*"Then Jesus, **looking at him, loved him, and said to him**, 'One thing you lack: Go your way, sell whatever you have and give to the poor, and you will have treasure in heaven; and come, take up the cross, and follow Me.'"* [1]

Know this: Jesus is looking at you and loving you.

What if His truth was only ministering to you for your freedom — not for your acceptance?

You are **already accepted** in the Beloved. [2]

When God knocks on a hidden door in our hearts, on a place needing surrender, we can want to run and hide, but the Lord says, "Do not fear. I'm not ministering truth to you so you can become a son. I'm ministering truth to you because you already are one!" [3]

Sons receive correction as an evidence of sonship, not as a means by which to achieve sonship.

Remember, when God is speaking truth into a difficult area, it is ONLY for your freedom, not for your acceptance. [4]

It's His goodness that leads us to repentance! [5]

God Sees You

Jesus saw the rich young ruler right where he was. The rich young ruler didn't like how Jesus saw through him, so he ran and hid just like Adam did. [6]

God responds to our honesty and humility. Pride tries to conceal what God wants to heal.

The enemy wants us to hide behind religious duty — to try to keep up our appearances before God; but Jesus says, *"Come to Me, all you who labor and are heavy laden, and I will give you rest."* [7]

When Adam and Eve sinned they sewed fig leaves. [8] They manufactured an image of themselves that they thought God wanted to see.

When the enemy tries to shame us we tend to put up an image, a front, saying, "God, I think you want to see me **this** way."

But "*the Scripture says, 'Whoever believes on Him will not be put to shame.'*"[9] God made it very clear that He was not pursuing Adam because Adam was able to hide his own nakedness; He was not after Adam because Adam had sewn some fig leaves. He actually wanted Adam just the way Adam was — without the fig leaves. Mess and all.

Adam couldn't believe that.

We have a hard time believing that God loves us just the way we are, but the truth is He wants connection with us right now, just the way we are!

We think we have to come to Him with a pious, righteous mindset. However, the Word says that your righteousness is as filthy rags before Him.[10] You're never going to be good enough, but He loves you anyway — completely.

That's why He sent Jesus to die on the Cross.[11]

Only God's Presence Can Cover Your Nakedness

God was used to spending time with Adam and Eve, talking with them in the midst of the Garden; but after eating from the Tree of the Knowledge of Good and Evil, when they heard the Lord, Adam and his wife hid themselves from His presence.[12] They began to use the resources God had given them (trees and creative ability) to hide from Him. They created a covering for their nakedness.[8] They hid behind the trees — anything to not let God see them in this state!

So, too, we often rely on our resources and personal strengths to create systems of hiding our own nakedness from ourselves and our Loving Creator. Some of us hide behind intellect or amazing relational abilities. Some of us hide behind material wealth or a gift for getting things done. Yet all the while, like Adam and Eve, we are hiding from the very One that is ready to cover us.

Only the presence of God can cover your nakedness.

God desires for you to be uncovered before Him. Even if you don't like what you see, He does not want you to create a version of yourself that you think will help Him accept you.

God wants each of His children to have an open conversation with Him.

God was calling out to His son, "Where are you, Adam? I know that you're hiding from me, but I'm the only one that can cover your nakedness." Adam replied, *I heard Your voice in the garden, and I was afraid because I was naked; and I hid myself.*[13]

You too may be feeling the Spirit of God speak to your heart right now, "Where are you? Can I please talk to the real you?"

You Will not Be Put to Shame

Peter didn't want to go back to the coals of his denial, but apart from Jesus meeting Him again at the coals by the Sea of Galilee, there would have been no opportunity for God to redeem Peter and reassure him of their relationship.[14]

Is your relationship with God completely open and totally free?

Do you have assurance before His presence? [15]

Or is there something that you're too afraid to let be known before Him? Something where you've not yet allowed yourself to hear His voice of love?

"I heard Your voice in the garden, and I was afraid because I was naked; and I hid myself." [13]

Too often we don't come to Him as children. We don't come to Him as our authentic selves. We present the religious versions of ourselves and God is waiting for us to get rid of that. He is saying, "Listen, when you're really willing to be real with Me and be yourself, I'll be able talk with you. I'll be able to show My love to you and you'll be able to know Me like you've always wanted to. But I don't want to talk to a stranger. I want to talk to my kid. And I know my kid."

For Adam, the fear came because of the shame. Shame believes the lie that the Father has turned His face away.[16] Shame believes God doesn't want to accept you. Shame tells you to hide.

But the shame is about to die.

Don't Cover It Up

The Father's love was inviting Adam out of hiding. So, too, the Father's love is inviting you. He wants to know the real you! Your adoption is not predicated on your performance. Your adoption is predicated on His love.[17] Like Adam, you have no need to hide.

"Then the Lord God called to Adam and said to him, 'Where are you?'" [18]

Adam could have responded differently to His Father's loving call, "I believed the lie about myself. I messed up. I ate from that Tree and now all I can see is my deficiency. But let me be naked before You."

God is asking us to expose our nakedness to Him.

The enemy lies to us, compels us to conceal and hide. "Do it in secret. Don't tell the truth. Cover it up." Sometimes without even realizing it, we find distractions to cover up our nakedness and need. We work our fingers to the bone for money or success, we cover it over with drinking or using, or we even avoid honest conversations with our Father by busying ourselves with trying to do good things for Him.

Don't conceal what God wants to heal.

Only the presence of God can cover your nakedness. Only the words of God can make you clean. God has given no avenue for purity apart from relationship with Him.

"I acknowledged my sin to You, and my iniquity I have not hidden. I said, 'I will confess my transgressions to the Lord,' and You forgave the iniquity of my sin." [19]

The Garden is for those who allow God to cover their nakedness.

"You will show me the path of life; in Your presence is fullness of joy; at Your right hand are pleasures forevermore." [20]

"Here I am, Lord ..."

10

"IN WHOSE PRESENCE
AM I STANDING?"

Discovering Our Purpose

We are still sewing fig leaves.

"Do not love the world or the things in the world. If anyone loves the world, the love of the Father is not in him. For all that is in the world — the lust of the flesh, the lust of the eyes, and the pride of life — is not of the Father but is of the world. And the world is passing away, and the lust of it; but he who does the will of God abides forever." [1]

The lust of the flesh, the lust of the eyes, and the pride of life describe the range of fig leaves we might sew. But if we're still sewing fig leaves — if we're still trying to cover our nakedness — we don't yet know the love of the Father.

Throughout human history, we unfortunately see the effects of corruption. 2 Peter 1 says that corruption is in the world due to lust, so everywhere there is corruption, there was first lust.[2] We also all know how common pride is — it is almost a presumed part of the human condition! Yet the good news is that for every lust problem, for every pride problem, for every ambition / drivenness problem, there is a Father's-love solution!

From Adam and Eve until now, it's still either the love of the Father or fig leaves. It's still either the love of the Father or lust and pride.

The Father's love says, "Bring your shortcomings before me — it's in your vulnerability that you'll be free."

There are two types of purposes in life: (1) Bringing ourselves continually before God, or (2) Trying to prove (validate) ourselves to others.[3]

The second type is the way of the world. When men praised Jesus He did not entrust Himself to man because He knew what was in man: the desire to be validated by others, instead of by the only One Who could truly cover their nakedness.[4]

Lust is attempted self-validation.

Obsession is unfulfilled lust.

Contentment is a lack of obsession.

Contentment is the fruit of God's validation.

Do not be conformed to the world.[5] The Gentiles seek after all those things.[6]

How Our Will Works

*"In Him we have redemption through His blood, the forgiveness of sins, according to the riches of His grace which He made to abound toward us in all wisdom and prudence, having made known to us **the mystery of His will, according to His good pleasure which He purposed in Himself.**"*[7]

Paul is revealing here **how** God's will works and what we see is a progression like this:

God's good pleasure / purpose → God's will

Again, the Greek for "according to" is *kata* which means "stemming forth from." God's will is coming from His good pleasure / purpose.

We see this same progression play out two verses later as well. *"In Him also we have obtained an inheritance, being predestined **according to the purpose of Him who works all things according to the counsel of His will.**"*[7]

Again we see that God's purpose leads to God's will and we also discover that God **works** all things according to (*kata*) the counsel of His will! So in total the will works like this:

God's good pleasure / purpose → God's will → God's actions

If this is how God's will works, and we are made in His image, we know how our will works too!

Our good pleasure / purpose → our will → our actions

In other words, your purpose determines your will and your will determines your actions. We work all things according to the counsel of our will!

The Counsel of our Will

The counsel of our will is so strong that it can actually block spiritual discernment. Jesus said, ***"If anyone wills to do His will, he shall know*** *concerning the doctrine, whether it is from God or whether I speak on My own authority."* [9]

In some areas of our life, we can't get to a renewed mind, because we don't yet have a surrendered will in that area.

Romans 12:2 famously says, *"And do not be conformed to this world, but be transformed by the renewing of your mind, that you may prove what is that good and acceptable and **perfect will of God**."*

But before we can renew our mind in verse 2, we must first present our bodies a living sacrifice in verse 1: *"I beseech you therefore, brethren, by the mercies of God, that you present your bodies a living sacrifice, holy, acceptable to God, which is your reasonable service."* A living sacrifice is characterized by continual surrender.

Surrender comes before not being conformed to this world. Surrender comes before being transformed by the renewing of your minds.

Your will is not a "thinker," but a "decider."

God's not exposing your thinking; He's revealing your purposes.

Presence Determines Purpose

Ephesians 1:11 reads *"according to the purpose of Him who works all things according to the counsel of His will ..."*

We know our purpose determines our will and our will counsels our actions, but let's dive into the word "purpose." The Greek word for "purpose" is *próthesis*. Amazingly, of its twelve uses in the New Testament, four times it is translated "showbread." The showbread was twelve cakes of fine flour (representing the people of God), which were set before the presence of the Lord at all times!

Do you see it?

Our purposes will always be determined by His presence!

This is even true in the natural as Proverbs 18:1 wisely describes: *"A man who **isolates himself** seeks **his own desire**."* People with ulterior motives usually work behind someone's back; they first isolate themselves in order to seek their own desire. Therefore, when we come out of hiding, we stand face-to-face with God and His presence causes our purposes and desires to change!

Every other audience we choose to stand before requires a certain type of covering and our purpose becomes producing that covering. When we come into the Father's presence and allow Him to cover our nakedness, we are no longer driven by the purpose of covering-our-own-nakedness.

So the main question is, "In whose presence are you standing?"

When we stand before God with our nakedness completely laid bare before Him, we are accepted in the Beloved and our hearts are assured of His love. Because His love covers over **everything**, there remains no other covering for us to seek.[11] The shame is gone and the love of the Father causes all the other motivators — the lust of the flesh, the lust of the eyes, and the pride of life — to simply melt away.

This is why Jesus told His disciples, *"Watch and **pray**, lest you enter into temptation. The spirit indeed is **willing**, but the flesh is weak."*[12]

When we stand before God's presence our purposes are changed!

Presence (audience) → purpose → will → actions

You were made to be covered by His presence. Garden living is for those who will surrender the pursuit of other coverings and allow God to cover their nakedness.

The purposes of God become our purposes in His presence.

"In whose presence
am I standing?"

11

"WATCH AND PRAY"

Struggling to Find the Will of God

Some of us struggle to find the will of God. Perhaps we doubt the very things He gives us, or we get distracted by things He has not given us.

In Romans 8 we read that *"For as many are led by the Spirit of God, these are the sons of God"* and if we are each honest with ourselves we may recognize that "there is a large portion of my days where I don't experience that sort of leading." [1]

Why, as sons of God, do we sometimes struggle to follow the lead of the Spirit of God? Why, as beloved children for whom God has prepared good works for us to walk in, do we sometimes struggle to find the will of God?

In Mark 3, Jesus asked a rhetorical question: *"Who is My mother, or My brothers?"* [2]

Jesus then proceeded to answer His own question for those who were present: *"He looked around in a circle at those who*

sat about Him, and said, 'Here are My mother and My brothers!
*For **whoever does the will of God** is My brother and My sister*
and mother.'" [3]

The reason we often struggle to hear the direction of God
is because we are not yet ready to surrender to His will. As
James says, we are "double-minded."

"If any of you lacks wisdom, let him ask of God, who gives to all
liberally and without reproach, and it will be given to him. But
let him ask in faith, with no doubting, for he who doubts is like
a wave of the sea driven and tossed by the wind. For let not that
man suppose that he will receive anything from the Lord; he is a
double-minded man, unstable in all his ways." [4]

Double-mindedness is like a child trying to chase two rabbits
at the same time. As the old saying goes, "chase one rabbit,
catch one; chase two rabbits, catch none." When we haven't
decided that we'll do what God tells us to, it can be tough
to hear what He's saying to do.

This may be why some of us are perpetually trying to "find
our purpose." This may be why some of us are forever trying
to stir up a passion for the work of God. Perhaps what we
haven't yet found is our surrender to His will. When our mind
becomes singular to hear His will on a matter, He will give
wisdom to each of us liberally and without reproach. He's
happy to lead those who are ready to follow Him, and that's
where we find our life!

"Then Jesus told his disciples, "If anyone would come after me, let him deny himself and take up his cross and follow me. For whoever would save his life will lose it, but whoever loses his life for my sake will find it." [5]

Wrestle with Your Will or Wrestle with God

Are you often tempted by something familiar? Yes, it could perhaps be some observable sin, but it could also be a temptation of the heart. Perhaps a temptation to pride or judgment, or even a temptation to fear or worry?

Sometimes temptation needs to be managed. For example, Proverbs 23 describes a situation with a need to manage temptation: *"When you sit down to eat with a ruler, consider carefully what is before you; and put a knife to your throat if you are a man given to appetite. Do not desire his delicacies, for they are deceptive food."* [6]

The scene Solomon is painting is of someone going to a royal palace or wealthy man's house and realizing they have an appetite / desire for the rich man's delicacies. Solomon exhorts that man to *"put a knife to your throat,"* or in other words, to exhibit self-restraint.

While there is an important place in a believer's life for self-restraint like Solomon described, if you are often tempted in a similar way, or you are continually needing to exhibit self-restraint in the same area, know that you are wrestling with your will.

Like James says, *"each one is tempted when he is drawn away by his own **desires** and enticed."* [7] Our desires and purposes determine our will, and we work all things (i.e., act) according to the counsel of our will. [8]

The reason the person who was going to eat with the ruler needed a knife for self-restraint is because he was managing an unyielded desire. If the desire had died, there wouldn't need to be the same sort of management.

Sin management often has to do with a lack of surrender. As a lifestyle, this can be debilitating as we often find ourselves unknowingly wrestling with our own will. The solution for the place of struggle is not to willpower your way through it without God, but instead to bring the struggle before God, have an open conversation with Him about it, and surrender your will to Him. Jesus did not wrestle with His will on His own – apart from His Father. Instead, at Gethsemane, He drew near to His Father and wrestled with God. [9] He exhorts us to handle temptation in the same way: *"Watch and pray, lest you enter into temptation. The spirit indeed is willing, but the flesh is weak."* [10] Prayer changes our audience, which changes our purposes, which starts to change who's counsel we are acting in accordance with.

We can either keep wrestling with our wills or start to wrestle with God (in prayer). Surrender changes our desires.

The Missing Food

Peter exhorts young believers to desire the pure milk of the word that they may grow thereby.[11]

The Word Himself, Jesus, says, *"I am the bread of life. He who comes to Me shall never hunger, and he who believes in Me shall never thirst."*[12]

God's word is spiritual food that nourishes us and causes us to grow.

Yet many of us, if we are honest, eat and eat and are never fully satisfied. We continually receive more revelation, more knowledge of God and His Word, yet something in us is still unsatisfied.

Perhaps we've eaten and not been satisfied because there's food we've not known about. Jesus is again saying to many of us, *"I have food to eat of which you do not know."*[13]

*"My food is **to do the will** of Him who sent Me, and to finish His work."*[14]

There is a satisfaction in surrender that causes the lust for more and ambition to fade away — and invites contentment to come! Contentment allows us to prosper in all things - whether we abound or are abased.[15] It will allow us to do the simple things thoroughly. Contentment's emphasis is on here, not there. Contentment positions us to be able **to do** all things through Christ Who strengths us.[16]

*"I have learned in whatever state I am, to be **content**: I know how to be abased, and I know how to abound. Everywhere and in all things I have learned both to be full and to be hungry, both to abound and to suffer need. I can **do** all things through Christ who strengthens me."* [17]

God's will for your life is not out of reach for you today. God has prepared good works for you to walk in; when we are faithful with little, we are given more. [18]

*"'Well done, good servant; because you were **faithful** in a very little, have authority over ten cities.'"* [19]

Faithfulness is fulfilling. Proverbs says, *"The fear of the Lord leads to life, and he who has it will **abide in satisfaction**."* [20]

"For I have come down from heaven, not to do My own will, but the will of Him who sent Me." [21]

To Will and to Do

There is a difference between teachings and trainings – and the difference is not in the content of what is shared. The difference is in the heart of the hearer.

A training is simply a teaching that is received by someone who is willing to act. Trainings are teachings for action.

The church has struggled in some teaching settings because the amount of information shared is beyond the audience's willingness for action.

In thinking about discipleship, some of us are truth-limited. That looks like powerlessness or ineffective ministry. The Word of God thoroughly equips us for every good work.[22]

Some of us are love-limited. That looks like not having access to people's hearts. No one cares what you know until they know that you care.[23]

But many of us are obedience-limited. That looks like being a hearer of the word, but not a doer of the word that we've heard.[24]

Paul exhorts us to *"work out your own salvation with fear and trembling; for it is God who works in you both **to will** and **to do** for His good pleasure."*[25]

To will.

and

To do.

*"My food is **to do the will** of Him who sent Me, and to finish His work."*[14]

Jesus first wrestled with God to surrender His will in Gethsemane, and then He walked out that surrender the next day on Calvary.[26]

The **doing** comes from the **willing**. The willing comes from the wrestle and the surrender.

Each of us must work out our **own** salvation with fear and trembling. God will work in you both **to will** and **to do** for His good pleasure.

"The spirit indeed is willing ..." [27]

Watch and pray.

"Watch and pray."

CHAPTER NOTES

Introduction

1. Lk. 10:1
2. Ez. 3:3-4
3. Jn. 17:3
4. Rom. 12:2
5. Phil. 2:12

Foreword

1. Isa. 60:3
2. Jn. 18:10
3. Jn. 18:15-26
4. Jn. 21:19
5. Jn. 20:11-18
6. Gen. 3:1-7
7. Mt. 26:36-46
8. Jn. 2:1-12

Chapter 1. God is Working in the Will of His People

1. Mt. 26:38
2. Gen. 3:22-24
3. Mt. 4:1-11
4. Mt. 26:36-46
5. Mt. 17:1-9
6. Mt. 26:39
7. Mt. 26:40
8. Mt. 26:41
9. Ps. 46:10
10. Mt. 26:40
11. Ex. 33:11
12. Jn. 5:19, para.
13. 2 Cor. 3:18
14. Jn. 15:7
15. Mt. 26:39
16. Mt. 26:42,44

Chapter 2. It's a Choice

1. Mt. 26:36
2. Mt. 26:36-46
3. Jn. 15:7
4. Mt. 6:9-10
5. Gen. 2:24-25
6. Mt. 19:4-6
7. Rev. 19:6-9
8. Jn. 3:16

9. Gal. 2:20
10. Jn. 10:17-18a
11. Rom. 8:7
12. Rom. 12:2
13. e.g., Eph. 4:26
14. Phil. 2:12-13
15. Mt. 26:39,42,44

Chapter 3. Knowing God is not a Means to Another End

1. Phil. 2:13-15
2. James 4:1
3. Rom. 12:18
4. Ps. 32:2
5. Isa. 57:15
6. Mt. 5:3
7. Lk. 9:24
8. Ps. 37:4
9. Mt. 7:21-23 (note v. 23 *"I never KNEW you ..."*)
10. Heb. 11:6
11. 1 Tim. 6:5
12. 1 Tim. 6:6
13. Mt. 16:4
14. Jn. 7:18
15. Jn. 17:22-23a
16. Jn. 17:3
17. Jn. 14:23
18. Jn. 17:23

19. Mk. 4:21

20. Ps. 27:4

21. Phil. 3:7-8 (note: don't miss vv. 9-11 as well!)

22. Prov. 1:23

Chapter 4. It's Between You and God

1. Jn. 15:14

2. Jn. 6:12 (and vv. 1-14 for the full account)

3. Jn. 6:14

4. Jn. 15:15

5. See Lk. 11:52 and Mt. 23:12-13

6. 2 Peter 3:15-16

7. Acts 9:6

8. Acts 9:5

9. Lk. 6:46

10. Acts 9:3-18

11. Jn. 10:27

12. The Greek of the word Nicolaitans (*Nikolaitēs*) means "destruction of people, victor over the people, subdue people or conquer." In Revelation 2, Jesus twice says He hates the doctrine of the Nicolaitans. The way the Nicolaitans had victory over people was through false teaching. According to the early church fathers the Nicolaitans preached a doctrine of compromise and they made people believe that it's acceptable to serve idols and God. We have drawn a connection between their doctrine (which inserted someone or something between God and man) and what Jesus says He will give those who repent and overcome it: a white stone which has *"a new name written which no one knows except him who receives it."*

13. Rev. 2:17

14. Heb. 8:10b-11
15. Acts 1:8; 1 Jn. 5:9-10
16. Phil. 2:13
17. Rev. 12:11
18. 1 Cor. 2:1-5 speaks to the importance of demonstration of the Spirit and power. Paul said, *"And my speech and my preaching were not with persuasive words of human wisdom, but in demonstration of the Spirit and of power, that your faith should not be in the wisdom of men but in the power of God."*
19. Jn. 7:17
20. Jn. 5:30; Prov. 23:7
21. Acts 8:1-3
22. 1 Cor. 4:19-20
23. Rom. 14:12

Chapter 5. It is God Who Works in You to Will

1. Ps. 107:9
2. 1 Thes. 5:16-18
3. 1 Thes. 5:19-22
4. 1 Thes. 5:23-24
5. 1 Peter 5:7
6. Jn. 6:28
7. Jn. 6:29
8. Gal. 3:3
9. Jn. 6:63
10. Rom. 4:3
11. Rom. 8:1
12. See Gal. 5:16-25

13. Rom. 8:5-6
14. See Gal. 5:1-6
15. Jn. 3:16
16. Mt. 26:41
17. Eph. 2:8-9
18. Jn. 1:12 and 1 Jn. 3:1
19. Eph. 1:4b-6
20. Heb. 12:7-8
21. Jn. 8:32
22. Rom. 2:4

Chapter 6. Whatever It Is, It's Readily Available in Him

1. Jn. 15:3
2. Prov. 20:9
3. Lk. 15:18b-19
4. See Rom. 5:20
5. Mt. 26:41
6. Jude 24
7. Hab. 1:13
8. Hab. 2:2-4
9. This verse is also referenced 3 times in the NT (Rom. 1:17; Gal. 3:11; and Heb. 10:38)
10. 1 Tim. 1:15
11. Lk. 2:7-14
12. Mt. 11:19
13. Rom. 5:8-9
14. See 1 Jn. 3:1
15. Isa. 41:9b

16. Gen. 3:9

17. See 1 Jn. 4:18

18. 1 Jn. 2:16

19. Lk. 15:13

20. Lk. 15:22-27

21. See Mt. 7:7-11

22. See Eph. 3:20-21

23. See James 1:16-17

Chapter 7. "Everything You Need is Found in Me"

1. 1 Peter 5:6-7

2. Mt. 7:11

3. 2 Peter 1:3

4. Ex. 3:14

5. This is where corruption came into the world through lust (see 2 Peter 1:4), which caused creation to be subjected to futility (see Rom. 8:19-21).

6. Gen. 2:8-9

7. Gen. 2:16-17

8. Jn. 14:6

9. Jn. 15:5

10. See Jn. 15:4-8

11. James 1:16-17

12. Prov. 14:12; Prov. 16:25

13. Mt. 19:16-17a

14. Mt. 19:21

15. Mt. 6:21; Lk. 12:34

16. Mt. 19:22

Chapter 8. "I Surrender"

1. 2 Sam. 12:1-5

2. 2 Sam. 12:6

3. 2 Sam. 12:7a

4. Having "ears to hear" is a matter of the heart -- an issue of humility and surrender. Originally, the phrase was from Ezekiel 12:2 which says, *"Son of man, you dwell in the midst of a rebellious house, which has eyes to see but does not see, and ears to hear but does not hear; for they are a rebellious house."* Notice that rebellion had caused them to have eyes to see that couldn't actually see and ears to hear that couldn't actually hear. There are eight places in the Gospel where Jesus decrees *"He (or 'anyone') who has ears to hear, let him hear!"* Each time He declares it with an exclamation point! The point is simple but essential: the state of our heart determines what we really hear. In the New Covenant, God has replaced our old stony hearts and has given us hearts of flesh so that He can write upon them (Ez. 36:26; 2 Cor. 3:3; and Heb. 8:10).

5. Ps. 32:9

6. 1 Tim. 6:6

7. 1 Tim. 6:7

8. Jn. 5:19

9. Jn. 12:49

10. 2 Cor. 1:20

11. Rom. 4:17

12. Jer. 29:11, ESV

13. Notice Jesus' leadership development plan for His twelve apostles in Mk. 3:13-15; *"And He went up on the mountain and called to Him those He Himself wanted. And they came to Him. Then He appointed twelve, that they might be with Him and that He might send them out to preach, and to have*

power to heal sicknesses and to cast out demons ..." The first step was *"**that they might be with Him**."* He knows that when we are **with** Him we will accomplish His purposes.

14. Ps. 27:4
15. See Jn. 15:5
16. Ps. 107:9
17. Phil. 4:7

Chapter 9. "Here I Am, Lord ..."

1. Mk. 10:21
2. Eph. 1:6
3. See Heb. 12:5-11
4. See Jn. 8:31-32
5. Rom. 2:4
6. Mk. 10:22
7. Mt. 11:28
8. Gen. 3:7
9. Rom. 10:11
10. Isa. 64:6
11. See 2 Cor. 5:21
12. Gen. 3:8
13. Gen. 3:10
14. Jn. 21:5-22
15. See Heb. 10:19-23
16. In Numbers 12:14, the Lord spoke to Moses about Miriam's rebellion and said *"If her father had but spit in her face, would she not be **shamed** seven days?"* It appears the idea of shaming was not just a feeling, but instead an actual disgraceful removal from the presence of the father. The priestly blessing God told Aaron and his sons to pray

over the children of Israel speaks the opposite of shame —*"The LORD bless you and keep you; **the LORD make His face shine upon you**, and be gracious to you; the LORD lift up His countenance upon you, and give you peace"* (Num. 6:24-26). As a born-again believer, Jesus is now your High Priest and He is blessing you to see how your Heavenly Father's face lights-up (shines) when He sees you!

17. See Rom. 8:15-16
18. Gen. 3:9
19. Ps. 32:5
20. Ps. 16:11

Chapter 10. "In Whose Presence am I Standing?"

1. 1 Jn. 2:15-17
2. 2 Peter 1:4
3. See Gal. 1:10
4. See Jn. 2:23-25
5. See Rom. 12:2
6. Mt. 6:32
7. Eph. 1:7-9
8. Eph. 1:11
9. Jn. 7:17
10. There are many verses about the showbread, but Ex. 25:23-29 and Lev. 24:5-9 are good places to start.
11. 1 Peter 4:8
12. Mt. 26:41; Mk. 14:38

Chapter 11. "Watch and Pray"

1. Rom. 8:14
2. Mk. 3:33

3. Mk. 3:34-35
4. James 1:5-8
5. Mt. 16:24-25, ESV
6. Prov. 23:1-3
7. James 1:14
8. See Eph. 1:7-9, 11
9. Mt. 26:36-46
10. Mt. 26:41
11. 1 Peter 2:2
12. Jn. 6:35
13. Jn. 4:32
14. Jn. 4:34
15. Phil. 4:12
16. Phil. 4:13
17. Phil. 4:11b-13
18. See Eph. 2:10 and Lk. 16:10
19. Lk. 19:17
20. Prov. 19:23
21. Jn. 6:38
22. 2 Tim. 3:16-17
23. 1 Cor. 13:1-3
24. James 1:22-25
25. Phil. 2:12b-13
26. Mt. 26:36 – 27:56
27. Mk. 14:38

ABOUT THE AUTHORS

Danny Ortiz

Danny Ortiz is a husband of 23 years to his beloved wife Debbie and a father to three incredible young ladies. Danny, Debbie and the girls love to travel and see the world through the eyes of others. Born and raised in the South Bronx, New York, Danny experienced first-hand the challenges and difficulties of being raised in the inner city, and he has a passion to minister to families. In ministry for over 28 years, Danny has traveled across the nation and around the world preaching and teaching a message of awakening and reformation to see people come to know Jesus intimately. As a pastor, business consultant, and leadership mentor, he carries a unique gift that helps individuals to grow in spirit, soul, and body, so that they can fulfill Matthew 22:37-39, "love God and love people."

Inquiries: info@dannyortiz.org

Peter DeWitt

Peter is a husband to Megan, and a father to Peter (III), Andrew, David and William. His background is in education, having served first as a science teacher, then as an administrator, and now as a consultant. Peter's wife, Megan, led him to the Lord while they were both in college at Ohio State, a time where Peter mostly rock climbed and sometimes studied! Peter has since enjoyed freedom after freedom in the Lord as he has experienced more and more of God's great love for him. As a pastor, consultant, and resource creator, Peter is called to assist in mobilizing ministers in every sphere of culture through kingdom-focused mentorship, perspective, and articulation. As a family, the DeWitt's enjoy tasty food, hiking, fly fishing, and summertime baseball and swimming.

Connect with Peter on Facebook: http://fb.com/PeterDeWitt55

Inquiries: info@peterdewitt.org